From Rehab to Recovery
the truth about getting clean
and staying clean, in spite of ourselves

by
Janice L. Witt, M.A.
Addiction and Trauma Specialist

The Author has strived to be as accurate and complete as possible in the writing of this book, notwithstanding the fact that she does not warrant or represent, at any time, that the contents within are accurate due to the changing nature of addiction treatment.

While all attempts have been made to verify information provided in this book, the Author assumes no responsibility for errors, ommissions, or contrary interpretation of the subject matter herein. Any perceived slights of specific individuals, peoples, or organizations are unintentional.

This book is not intended for use as a source for medical advice. All readers are advised to seek the services of a medical professional or addictionologist when making decisions about substance abuse and addiction treatment.

Contact the Author:

Janice L. Witt
P.O. Box 10758
Prescott, AZ 86304

www.BrainandBeing.com
support@brainandbeing.com

ISBN: 978-1494255831

For all of my people,
all over the world,
looking for new and better ways of living -
You can find them!

TABLE OF CONTENTS

FOREWORD

To the Parents, Husbands, Wives, and loved ones of those who suffer with the disease of addiction.

"I'm at the end of my rope." "I don't know what to do anymore." "Every word out of his mouth is a lie."

"I feel like I'm trapped, like it's my fault." "She seems fine for awhile, then it all falls apart again." "She's promised me that it's over, that she'll never drink again." "I feel crazy. I search her purse and her car. I'm always looking for something. I don't even know what I'm looking for."

Sound familiar? These are the words that echo through addicted families. Desperate and frightened, those who love addicted people suffer tremendously. There are few diseases that ravage the lives of all those surrounding it like addiction does. The families who live with it feel shame, guilt, and an overwhelming sense of fear.

"Will my husband die?" "I think my wife is losing her mind." "My son's best friend just died of an overdose. Is my son next?"

Let's start at the beginning. Is addiction a disease? Yes! It has signs and symptoms. It's progressive in nature. It's chronic, and it often leads to death. Addiction also responds to treatment, and people do find remission or recovery.

In fact, I find no difference between the disease of cancer and the disease of addiction; except for the way our society views addiction. And this is a huge problem. We live in a culture that refuses to see this illness as a disease, and then, as a matter of course, refuses to effectively treat this life-threatening condition.

It's important to remember that no addict or alcoholic ever dreamed of becoming a drug addict when he or she was a child. Addiction is not a choice, and addicts feel trapped in their own shame, not knowing how to get out of their desperate states. Here is the prevailing theory of addiction, and it is important to consider:

Science believes that there is a genetic component to this disease. They've isolated the gene for Type II. Alcoholism, and believe that there are perhaps polygenic phenomena involved in the complexities of addiction theory, and this would include process addictions *(eating disorders, sex addiction, love addiction, compulsive gambling, and compulsive spending)*.

There is also the trauma aspect of addiction. All addictive disorders begin with something known as attachment disorder or attachment trauma. This condition occurs in utero and continues throughout the first 18 months of life *(More about attachment trauma in chapter 2)*. Attachment trauma is also compounded by various childhood experiences *(emotional abuse, physical abuse, and sexual abuse)*, not to mention bullying, rejection, and neglect. Later, after the addiction has taken hold, there are multitudinal traumas that take place as a result of the lifestyle addicts are forced to participate in, to enable their addictions to survive.

Next, as a result of the issues above, there are mental, emotional, and learning disabling states that need medication. What we've seen over time, is that the drug of choice that an addict is drawn to, is in direct correlation to the depression, anxiety, mood swings, and attentional deficits that were created years before.

This book addresses all of these issues, with research-based opinions regarding what kind of treatment works best and for whom.

I welcome you to learning more about the disease of addiction and then in advocating on the behalves of those who suffer from it.

Thank you.
Janice L. Witt, M.A.
Addiction and Trauma Specialist

Chapter One

WHERE IS THE EXIT SIGN?

"Where do I go for help? When I get online and look for treatment centers in Lansing, Michigan I get sent to some place in Florida. Why does this happen and is there treatment where I live?"

Yes! However, it is not as easy to find as one would think. With the extraordinary search engine Google, there has been an explosion of Search Engine Optimization people *(SEOs)* building sites to redirect your inquiries. The best place to look is on the National Institute on Drug Abuse's *(N.I.D.A.)* website: www.drugabuse.gov. They have a relatively up-to-date list of treatment centers in the United States, with listings by States and then Cities.

The next step is to know something about what you need. Are you looking for treatment for yourself? For your teenager? Young adult? Partner? Husband? Wife? Sister? Does your insurance cover treatment? *(Call now and find out).* Do you have the money to pay for treatment? What does treatment cost? Are you eligible for financing? *(And yes there is financing for addiction treatment).*

"Does paying more make a difference? How long is the right amount of time to stay in treatment? Are 30 day programs effective? Is there such a thing as free treatment?"

Next, does money matter? I'm going to answer this honestly. High-end treatment *(if research-based and proven)* is much better treatment than county-funded treatment or those in the $10,000. per month range. When treatment costs vary from $30,000., $45,000. up to $90,000. per month, the facility is considered high-end. The good ones are not country clubs. They do an excellent job at creating a highly skilled team of experts to help your loved one get well. And by and large, people get well and stay well in much higher numbers. This is the benefit of working with the best. Addictionologists *(Psychiatrists and MDs with board certifications in addiction medicine)*—Psychotherapists who specialize in trauma, addiction, and family systems therapy—Life coaches who understand where the developmental stop gaps are in addiction, and who can also help addicts move forward after treatment—Expressive Art Therapy, Equine Therapy, Somatic Experiencing, EMDR, and Neurofeedback are but some of the exceptional offerings in high-end facilities. Of course this isn't even including massage, cranial-sacral therapy, and the exquisite cuisine. All of which help people heal. And to remind you: Healing is the point.

When shopping for treatment centers, look for those that are research-based. Make sure the Therapist working with you or your loved one is at least a Master's level clinician. Note: It has become a popular practice within the addiction field to hire people who are in recovery and to call them therapists *(often these workers are considered Behavioral Health Technicians/ BHTs).* Many BHTs do not even hold Bachelor's degrees. This is a disaster in the making. Make sure that if they are called therapists, they are indeed therapists, trained in trauma, addiction treatment, and neuroscience.

Be certain that the treatment center is well-staffed. A 5:1 client to staff ratio would be the minimum amount of supervision acceptable. Drug testing is a must—do not send someone suffering from addiction to a center that does not concern itself with drug testing. Also, try to find a facility that utilizes neurofeedback *(see chapter 3 on Neurofeedback and addiction treatment)*. The long-term results are impressive.

Additionally, you are looking for a facility that employs at least one addictionologist/ and or a psychiatrist well-versed in addiction medicine. Spirituality is also an essential part of long term recovery. Please make sure that there are vehicles for spiritual growth in the program. Moreover, a 12-step component is an important ingredient of treatment—don't choose a facility that does not involve some kind of 12 step activity *(more on this in chapter 5)*.

If you or your loved one is in need of treatment, don't settle for a sober living because of cost—choose a licensed treatment facility.

A sober living facility is a transitional living opportunity for those who have successfully completed treatment. Shop well for these too, as many are not run well. In a transitional support community, you're looking for reliable staff, nutritional food, a clean environment, and a relatively large degree of structure. Also, don't accept a sober living that does not regularly drug test. Sober living facilities are notorious for allowing addicts to get high, while the owners turn a blind eye to the drug use in pursuit of a rent check.

No cost or extremely low cost treatment is available. It is rare. You will find it in larger cities and places that devote a significant amount of tax dollars to mental health and wellness. There are also religious programs committed to drug treatment that have low fees. The county programs, that do exist, do a darn good job with the budgets they have to work with. Having said that, most stays are between 30-45 days, and the people these facilities serve are the ones who need the longest possible treatment stays to recover and reenter life. Often, but not always, these centers are working with addicts who have fallen to the bottom of our societal structure: the homeless, severely and persistently mentally ill, prostitutes, and ex-convicts. They clearly need a great deal of time to find their ways back to themselves. This points to our need *(as a country)* to reevaluate how we see this disease, and the obvious present necessity for lobbying and rallying to obtain appropriate medical care for addicts.

"What about outpatient treatment?"

Often, insurance companies will want an addict to begin with an outpatient program, and then reevaluate if there is a relapse. Outpatient programs that offer substantial treatment can also be hard to find. Even so, they exist. Various monitoring programs with extensive drug testing, mandatory meetings, and effective group therapies do a good job. This would include the drug courts. I think the thing to remember, when choosing an outpatient facility, is that this type of treatment works best for those who are highly motivated to change *(often due to threats of losing their licenses or going to prison)* or for those who have not had to contend with years of ongoing addiction. If your insurance will only cover outpatient treatment in the beginning, give it your best shot; however, if relapse occurs, try a higher level of care—no different than an oncologist treating a leukemia patient— if the cancer returns—choose a higher dose of treatment.

30 days of treatment is not enough time to help a person get well! Addicts are only beginning to come down from drugs at 30 days. Going back to their previous lives after a month of treatment is almost certainly a recipe for relapse. This is predictable. Addicts need time and space away from the substances themselves, as well as from the environments in which they drank and used. *(High-end centers will frequently take clients for 30-day stays. Even so, they will encourage clients*

to stay on for step-down levels of care, knowing that recovery takes time. And often, these step-down levels are much less expensive than the initial 30 days of treatment.)

If you are looking for responsible addiction treatment, look for no less than 90 days. And yes, I know how difficult it can be to take someone out of his or her job or school for 3 months; even so, please don't consider less than 90 days. That would appear to be the minimum amount of time associated with successful treatment. Next, are you trying to help your young adult *(aged 18-27)*? Then, don't consider less time than 6 months. In fact, if the resources are available, it's been shown that 12-18 months is the most effective course of treatment for young adults, needing to launch in life without the aid of drugs. The necessity for a longer period of time, in a community setting, is much more pronounced with this group than in older populations.

Chapter Two

Attachment Disorder and Addiction

These insights are due to the tireless research and specializations of the following: Dr. Daniel Siegel, Dr. Daniel Stern, Dr. T. Berry Brazelton, Dr. Allan Schore, Dr. Gabor Mate, Dr. Stephen Porges, Mary Main, Dr. John Bowlby, Mary Ainsworth, Sir Richard Bowlby, and the Boston Change Group. I thank all of you for what you have brought to the fields of Neuroscience, Infant Brain Development, Attachment, Psychoanalysis, and Addiction.

In a little over a month, I'll have been in the field of addiction for 24 years. There have been some very important forward movements during the last 15-20 years in a field that has baffled human kind since Seneca first brought us wine. We've found a limbic connection in the brains of people affected by addiction. With the Human Genome Project, we've explored the, long hypothesized, genetic correlation to addiction, *(interesting findings regarding Type II. Alcoholism)*. For the longest time, we insisted that trauma, most probably sexual, was at the root of addiction. Then eventually we were forced to let that theory go, based on the experiences of our clients *(although there were some startling studies done with female addicts in treatment during the 80s that pointed heavily to sexual trauma)*. We explored family systems and found some credence to the idea that family backgrounds are predictors of future addiction issues; but still, this theory didn't fit everyone *(not even most)*. At this time, the prevailing theory looks like this:

- Genetic Predisposition
- Major Life Trauma *(Attachment trauma and then anything that occurs afterwards)*
- A substance that works to make life bearable

Attachment disorder or attachment trauma is one of the 3 fundamental building blocks of addiction. What research and experience have taught us is that those who are affected by such trauma can be found in populations suffering with PTSD, personality disorders, and addictions. More importantly, attachment is the ground in which addicts grow. Note: Adoptees, almost always have attachment disorders. When speaking of attachment disorders, I am not referring to Reactive Attachment Disorder, the clinical diagnosis from the DSM IV., which is a form of attachment disorder but is not reflective of the above groups.

This is how I explain attachment disorder/ trauma to my clients:

In utero, something happens for Mom. It could be that she is having a difficult physical pregnancy and feels sick or is bed-ridden. Maybe she and Dad aren't getting along, or maybe Dad is away in the military—deployed. It could be that she's had a miscarriage in the past and is terrified of losing this child, or that there are already 4 children, and how will she feed and care for a 5th? It could be that she is considering adoption or abortion. Mom's parents could be ill, or there might be financial problems. The mommy might have unaddressed attachment trauma from her own early childhood *(that was passed down to her from her mother)*, or she might be depressed. Really, it could be any one of a hundred things. Mom could have a drug problem or be an alcoholic, drinking or not drinking *(which can cause considerable anxiety)*. Dad could be the unreliable alcoholic that she is worried about. Again, it could be almost any one thing or combination of things. And this is during the time when the blueprint for the baby's emotional brain *(the right brain)* is being developed. Whatever Mommy is feeling becomes the foundation for what the baby's emotional life will become.

Then Baby is born, and Mommy puts into Baby everything she is feeling, right brain to right brain, through the eyes and through mirror neurons found in the frontal lobe. These feelings become the baby's emotional experience during the first 18 months of life *(When the right brain is developing)*. The left brain has not even come on board yet. Also, it is during this first 18-month period when the capacity for joy is developed. If there is not the needed happy, loving, mommy-baby dance, if mommy is anxious or depressed *(post-partum depression)*, if she has an attachment disorder *(quite common)*, or if Baby is adopted, those neurons are pruned.

Here is what I've learned from my clients over the course of 24 years:

Alcoholics and people who are addicted to benzodiazepines are hard-wired for anxiety—no exceptions. Their first drink *(or pill)* is a miracle for their anxious emotional states. There may also be depression *(as alcohol is a central nervous system depressant)*; or depression could be co-occurring from early attachment states. Alcohol is an incredible anti-anxiety drug. In fact, the brain learns that this substance is the answer to crippling anxiety, even after the alcohol begins to create devastating results for the alcoholic.

Opiate *(narcotic painkillers)* and Heroin addicts are depressed. They fall somewhere on the continuum from severe depression to dysthymia *(Dysthymia being a mild form of depression—a state of living in which there is no joy, excitement or passion)*. Think about it. The neurons for joy have been pruned during their emotionally formative early life. Depression is going to result. There is no better antidepressant than opiates. Culturally, we don't consider this when we talk about the war on drugs or the blight of heroin addiction affecting our young people. These addicts have found relief that they have desperately needed to survive. It bears thinking about.

Methamphetamine Addicts, in overwhelming numbers, have severe ADD/ADHD and are trying to self-medicate. For many, amphetamines are the first experience of clarity and focus. It's as if they have been living in a fog of confusion prior to this. That the drug causes psychosis and death are minor considerations for the person feeling intellectual prowess for the first time in his or her life. And in truth, they all believe that those dire consequences won't happen to them, because they are feeling more in control and more intelligent than they have ever felt. ADD/ADHD is also a frontal lobe issue, and has everything to do with infant brain development. Attachment is an issue here as well.

Marijuana addicts *(The heavy users—chronically smoking)* have issues of rage that the drug has kept at bay. Eventually, the drug ceases to work anymore; however this can take years to occur. But when it stops working, the rage is unstoppable. These are generally addicts who come from families where identity development has not been encouraged and where anger is not an acceptable emotion. They comply by not feeling their feelings, and self-medicating themselves into complacency and acceptability.

When a client tells me his or her drug of choice is crack cocaine, I assess for Bipolar I, Bipolar II, or Bipolar III. There is no evidence that Bipolar Disorder is in anyway associated with attachment problems. It appears to be physiological; however, the addiction does point to attachment issues, and cocaine is the drug most commonly used to medicate Bipolar disorder if the client is an addict.

With hallucinogens, there is often a propensity toward psychosis prior to the drug use. These are likely people with a predisposition for schizophrenia or schizoaffective disorder. It's important that they are carefully assessed after they've cleared from the drugs. Also, there are those who are called to a spiritual path and believe they will find what they're looking for with the aid of psychedelics. *(however, based on my observations, this would only be about 10% of hallucinogen users).*

Among the clients capable of accurate self-reporting or those equipped with the information from their mothers and fathers, I can connect their drugs of choice with early attachment trauma and emotional states that their mothers were going through.

Moreover, we know that complex trauma and/or personality disorders are attachment related, as is PTSD. Not only that, approximately 40% of addicts *(or more)* have some form of personality disorder. What Mary Main and Daniel Siegel teach us is that the cycle of attachment trauma can be broken: One only needs to make sense of his or her life to break the pattern. I recommend *Parenting from the Inside Out: Siegel and Hartzell*

Chapter Three

Neurofeedback for PTSD and Addiction

Trauma:

Trauma (whether from a one-time dramatic event or from a repetitive type, stemming from childhood) causes the central nervous system *(CNS)* to be on high alert. Whether the event/ events took place today or years ago, the brain has changed to accommodate that traumatic experience. It's as if a robber has come into a house causing panic in the residents of the home. The family *(in the house)* all experience an emergency response to the event. Yet for the person who has PTSD or lasting symptoms from trauma, he or she experiences that robber, in his or her brain every day. The metaphorical robber never leaves the system. The stress from the event is part of a continual loop that raises stress hormones, anxiety levels, and hypervigilance. Even though the incident presents no current danger or threat, the CNS cannot escape the experience. So a person can acknowledge something on a conscious level as having happened in the past, and that person will still be unable to convince the brain and the CNS that the trauma is not occurring in the present moment. It's as confounding as it is painful for those who suffer. Trauma, without intervention, will remain trapped in the right brain *(affecting the limbic system, and the frontal lobe)*, assaulting its host without mercy and causing damage to the brain.

PTSD:

Post Traumatic Stress Disorder *(PTSD)* occurs in approximately 10% of those who have been subjected to traumatic events which are outside the range of everyday life experience. This 10% is made up of people who have an attachment trauma *(disorder)* which takes place during the first 18 months of life. Afterwards, these people become vulnerable to trauma which could include: abuse *(physical, emotional, or sexual)*, accidents, witnessing something horrific, receiving shocking news, exposure to combat, or unrelenting grief. PTSD can also be a result of ongoing child neglect or stress.

The symptoms of trauma and PTSD can vary from states of extreme hypervigilance with anxiety, disturbing nightmares, exaggerated startle responses, and social withdrawal. Painful memories, intrusive thoughts, and flashbacks are also recurring symptoms of PTSD. Dissociation is one of the most common defense mechanisms that occurs with trauma. And due to this, those who have it can only talk about the trauma in a dissociative state. Otherwise, the left-brain language for the right-brain phenomenon is not available. This makes talk therapy, often a retraumatizing experience for the one suffering from PTSD. Other issues often associated with trauma are insomnia, lack of focus and concentration, phobias, depression, alcoholism, addictions, mood lability, and unstable relational and behavioral patterns.

Whether it's the pioneering work of Dr. Eugene Peniston at the Veterans Administration Medical Center in Fort Lyons, Colorado, or Dr. Carol Manchester in Cincinnati, Ohio, there is new hope for those who have been held captive to traumatic events from the past. The brain can literally be trained out of the destructive brainwave loops that keep the PTSD active. Using effective Neurofeedback systems, such as Brainpaint™, we can permanently eliminate the symptoms of PTSD from our addicted clients who have suffered, many for the majority of their lives.

Neurofeedback Works—Brainpaint™ works best! Find a treatment center that uses it.

After a comprehensive assessment, the practitioner and the Brainpaint™ system design a set of protocols calculated to benefit the client suffering from a host of issues, including trauma. For addicts, Neurofeedback also reduces depression, anxiety, and insomnia with incredible results. The computer, then, offers auditory and visual feedback to encourage the client in generating more desirable brain rhythms. This "neuro-feed-back" actually guides the client into a more calm state. In fact, using the slow wave, alpha theta protocol, clients are in a deep state of relaxation in which they are able to integrate trapped trauma and difficult material from the right brain into the left brain where language and logic live. Clients begin to feel a tremendous sense of empowerment as they take back their lives.

Some studies suggest that 80% of PTSD symptoms are resolved by the 18th session of Neurofeedback. See EEG Info. and the accompanying YouTube video on Neurofeedback and Trauma.

Why Neurofeedback?

Neurofeedback addresses the source of the trouble—problematic brainwave activity that got stuck in a disruptive pattern due to trauma. Neurofeedback does not rely on drugs and other chemicals to mask or modify the symptoms. Neurofeedback does not need the client to "relive" the trauma in order to move past it *(which more often than not, retraumatizes the Client)*. Neurofeedback addresses each brain individually and effectively. See Bessel Van der Kolk's research on Neurofeedback and Trauma Treatment.

Addiction and Trauma:

All addicts and alcoholics come from attachment trauma *(like PTSD sufferers)*, as do those with personality disorders. This becomes foundational to any traumatic life experience that occurs afterward *(family of origin problems, child abuse, and violence)*. Therefore, the relational patterns, behavioral patterns, and defensive mechanisms that accompany addiction can be addressed with the Alpha Theta protocol, changing lifelong patterns of painful, unhealthy adaptations.

Perhaps most important:

In the 2005, UCLA addiction study, the results showed that 77% of clients in treatment, who received 43 sessions of Neurofeedback and attended a 12-step or faith-based program were still clean one year after treatment. Now that's a reason to find a treatment center that offers it. For more information on the treatment centers that utilize the Brainpaint™ System for Neurofeedback, go to: www.brainpaint.com

Chapter Four

What is Effective Therapy and Why is Group Treatment Necessary?

The best addiction treatment challenges traditional psychotherapeutic models for working with addicts. And, over time, we've learned *(as a field)* that addicts need positive reinforcement, and they also need to be accepted the way they are and encouraged to continue the growth process.

Nothing positive comes from the old confrontational model of addiction treatment. Offering shame, guilt, and criticism to addicts and alcoholics who are drowning in their own existing shame is simply not effective. In fact, it causes harm. And I would argue that it is nothing less than abuse.

The Change Model, Motivational Interviewing, and the Transtheoretical Model of Change *(or Stages of Recovery)* help addicts in treatment and their families to gain a better understanding of relapse, along with a shift in focus from denial to readiness. We, as a field, have found that simply waiting for an addict/alcoholic to "hit bottom" is a limitation that we and our treatment population cannot afford to continue, support, or allow.

What helps addicts grapple with the ambivalence and shame inherent in their disease?

Cutting edge treatment facilities believe that clients need to be met where they are at, and that each individual will have his or her own perspective and relationship with the addiction itself.

The Five Stages of Change are:
1. **Precontemplation**
2. **Contemplation**
3. **Preparation**
4. **Action**
5. **Maintenance**

Precontemplation is the stage in which the desire to change addictive patterns does not yet exist. Most people suffering from addiction in this stage completely deny their problems. In the *contemplation* stage, drug addicts are somewhat aware that they have a problem. Addicts realize that there may be a necessity to address their dilemma, but they have not made a commitment to action *(or treatment). Preparation* is the stage that utilizes this initial recognition of the problem and then encourages the needed behavioral changes necessary for individuals to begin getting well. Addicts who are in this stage intend to take action in the near future, but have not been able to summon this ability during the past year. The stage of *action* is one in which individuals adjust their behaviors, experiences, and environments in order to begin a new life without drugs. Action requires the most noticeable behavioral changes and requires tremendous commitment, time, and energy. *Maintenance* is the stage whereby addicts take daily actions to prevent relapse and strengthen the growth attained during the action stage. Addicts typically remain in the maintenance stage for years, while building new lives.

An excellent clinical staff will help clients through the stages of change using multimodalities and openness to self-expression. Effective treatment addresses the diverse needs of addicts. As you are looking for state of the art treatment, look for a facility that supports more proactive interventions and creates a concentration on motivational enhancement that will help clients to "take charge" of their ongoing wellness and their commitment to lifelong sobriety. Psychotherapy should help addicts to become more authentic while discovering the unique aspects of themselves that they can share with their community.

Why is treatment done in groups and what is group therapy?

Getting well alone or in individual therapy is nearly impossible. This disease affects the addict neurologically, physically, spiritually, psychologically, emotionally, and socially. Moreover, the shame levels are so high in the addicted population—they rarely trust and open to those who haven't been through what they've been through. Addiction is an isolating illness, and the importance of taking on life with small groups of others in "the same boat" cannot be overstated. This prepares the addicted person for living a full life after treatment. There should always be some people *(for the rest of the addict's life)* who "know what he or she has been through." It keeps the recovering person connected, safe, and with minimal shame out in the real world.

The purpose of this section is to discuss the techniques used in conducting effective group therapy. To begin with, let's look at some of the similarities within a good addiction treatment group. In addition to addiction, each member of the group has two things in common. First, before coming to the point of seeking treatment, the addict probably tried a do-it-yourself program in an effort to change. The second similarity is that it wasn't working. In fact, the addiction has continued to worsen over time. The basic assumption of group therapy is that a major reason for this failure is that the most determined efforts cannot change what cannot be seen. And clearly, there is a great deal that those new to treatment are not seeing clearly.

For this reason the main goals for effective group therapy are to:
- Discover that the members of the group are deeply feeling persons
- To identify the defenses that have prevented this discovery
- To gain understanding and insight on how each group member communicates and relates to others
- To practice new ways of communicating and problem-solving with others
- To learn and practice new ways of giving and receiving feedback in non-defensive and authentic ways

Feelings:

While dramatic change in behavior is the ultimate goal of group therapy, the immediate purpose is to see more accurately what needs to shift or change. This requires the addict to see and discover himself or herself at a feeling level.

First, the addict's behavior, in the past, may have been so opposed to his or her value system that considerable feelings of remorse and self-loathing may have manifested. Addicts, active in their addiction, often accumulate a pool of negative feelings with a variety of masks or defenses that prevent their discovery. This can begin with mild disapproval, and then grow into remorse, and ultimately a deep self-hatred. Statements such as, "I'm no good." or "the world would be better off without me," reflect these negative feelings and attitudes. Admitting feelings is an important part of the recovery process, one where the addict will begin to look at the destruction that his or her addiction/alcoholism has caused.

Being in touch with the hostile feelings addicts have had toward themselves and the sense of helplessness and hopelessness that accompany them, make this period a vital moving description of their addiction history instead of simply and abstract theory. Addicts begin to feel the chaotic vulnerability in their lives prior to arriving in treatment; however, they are rarely able to sustain this awareness for an extended period of time. One of the important functions of the group is to help members identify the defenses that have prevented this pivotal self-discovery.

Another reason for stressing feelings is that many of the character flaws that have disabled addicts, for years, are reflected in basic feeling states or attitudes. As a result of the conflict between value systems and behaviors, most addicts have formed rigid negative feelings states called "attitudes" toward themselves and others. Many have become one or more of the following archetypal patterns: hostile; angry; self-pitying; fearful; defiant; phony; arrogant; or superior. While these are represented as feelings, some have become so thoroughly a part of the psyche as to be attitudinal in nature. They substantially color the way addicts see life and react to it. No longer are they simply people who feel resentment. Addicts now become resentful people. They may discover that they are not simply people who feel self-pity, but they have become self-pitying. What was once a feeling has now hardened into an attitudinal posture, often referred to in 12-step programs as a character defect. If an addict is to change, he or she must first become his or her authentic self at a feeling level.

Furthermore, addicts may be severely out of touch with their feelings, particularly the ones that have been described. But as you will see, it is not just negative feelings that are hidden and controlled. Positive feelings of joy and love can also be locked away or blocked from developing by the same defenses that seek to prevent the negative feelings. While the main focus of group therapy is on identifying destructive negative feelings, the acceptance of these destructive feelings will also free the newly recovering person's positive feelings. In group therapy, "feelings are facts." "How does that make you feel?" is a question that clients hear frequently in group, in order to help them identify these facts.

Since feelings are likely novel to the new client in treatment, here are some feeling words that are used every day: mad, sad, glad, afraid, ashamed, and hurt. The addict's first task is to discover and identify these feelings in order to see clearly who he or she is and what needs to be changed. Acceptance of "what is" precedes change. Being able to observe distinctly and accept what is—is difficult, however, because people don't know that which they do not yet know. In many ways, all people are somewhat blind and self-deluded, but they don't realize it. Addicts, in particular, say things like, "I know who I am and where I'm going." Or the Classic: "I know what's best for me." The denial causes many to fall back into the same self-destructive behaviors that got them in treatment to begin with. The idea that self-delusion is a part of this disease is a key element basic to group therapy. The Johari Window illustrates four aspects of ourselves that group is designed to change.

OPEN	CLOSED
BLIND	UNCONSCIOUS

The Johari Window was created by two men: Joseph Luft and Harrington Ingham— They posited that each person has an "Open Window" which is the persona that he presents to the world—a "Closed Window" which is the information about the self that a person is aware of yet doesn't disclose to the outside world—a "Blind Window" with qualities which the people around him observe, yet the person himself is not able to see—and an "Unconscious Window" that is unknown to the self and others. It is one of the purposes of group therapy to become more "open" to closed material; to begin to understand "blind" spots and where they affect each individual and others; and to allow those brave discoveries to become "open," leaving room for unconscious material to filter into the "blind" and "closed" windows—the next process of the group work.

Feedback:

It takes courage to risk confronting another person with feedback. Addicts have often traded their honesty for the approval of others in the past. However, when they care about their fellow group members, *(and if they want them to be honest in return)* they must present them with accurate pictures of themselves. Many excellent treatment centers use some form of the feedback formula developed by Pia Mellody.

"When I hear You" or "see You"_____

"I make up that"_____

"And about that I feel"_____

We ask addicts to just "be" with the feedback they receive for 24 hours before responding.

EXAMPLES:

"When I hear your voice sound so sad, I make up that you're really missing your family." And about that I feel scared that you'll want to leave treatment and go home before you're ready. I also see that you're committed to self-awareness and have a desire to get well."

"When I see and hear you yell at your mother, I make up that you have a long-standing pattern of manipulating her with your anger. And about that I feel concerned and irritated."

In many groups, giving advice is discouraged, unless it is asked for. It's also a good idea in group, not to rest on assumptions. Group members can simply ask or check out what they might be assuming.

Some common defenses that may come up for group members after receiving feedback are:

Rationalizing	Quibbling	Defiance
Justifying	Debating	Attacking
Projecting	Arguing	Aggression

43

Blaming	Sparring	Withdrawing
Accusing	Questioning	Silence
Judging	Interrogating	Hyper-verbalizing
Moralizing	Switching Subjects	Intimidating
Intellectualizing	Denying	Threatening
Being Smug	Analyzing	Joking
Explaining	Arrogance	Agreeing
Theorizing	Minimizing	Complying
Generalizing	Evading	Acting Out

Many feel fearful about being vulnerable in group. It might be helpful to try on that feeling— let the group know. Keeping these feelings a secret tends to intensify them.

Commitments to Group Therapy

The following guidelines will help you or your loved one get the most out of therapy groups and improve communication with other clients.

- Speak in the first person—Instead of starting with "people feel..." or "you sound..." Try starting with "I feel..." This will give the group more of a sense of you, rather than a broad generalization.

- Speak directly to individuals—look and speak directly to others. If another person asks you, "How do you feel about Luis?" Turn to Luis and address that feeling.

- Be as honest as you can about your feel-ings and thoughts—there are no taboos on language, thoughts, feelings or ex-pressions in the group. Groups generally ask only that you respect one another and refrain from threatening language or violence.
- Be in the moment—if you are having feelings about something try and express those feelings, in an appropriate manner, at the earliest appropriate time. Concen-trate on what is going on now.
- Be aware of your own body language—your body is the most basic and tangible aspect of yourself. Your body is continu-ally giving you messages. Besides your body giving you messages of hunger and temperature, your body also con-veys your emotional state: The open and closed position of your limbs, seating of palms, feeling fidgety, or having a rapid heartbeat, rocking, a flushed face, and increased elimination needs all convey what you're feeling.
- Be as spontaneous as possible—You may find yourself mulling over what you want to say, choosing careful language, waiting to speak or trying to be polite. Instead, try

to let ideas, thoughts, and feelings flow freely, so the group can have the opportunity to find out more about the true you. Editing your thoughts and feelings often waters down and negates your freshness, sparkle, and genuineness.

- Be aware of the roles you take and your characteristic behavior—Individuals tend to behave similarly in many situations. For instance, you may have a tendency to be confrontational, while others in the same situation act withdrawn or even want to run away. Maybe you're the type who prefers to compromise or act as a peacemaker. Behavior in group therapy often mimics how you interact with significant others, friends, parents, and associates. By observing yourself and others in group, you will gain helpful insight into your interaction with others.

- Be aware of how individuals in the group may remind you of significant people in your life.

- Practice active listening—Give eye contact to those speaking; lean in; listen with your heart.

- Speak for yourself, not others

- Expect periods of silence—even though they may feel uncomfortable, use the silence that occurs in group to assess what you are feeling.

The importance of finding an appropriate fit for the person needing treatment is immense. Make sure that you're apprised about the quality of groups offered at the facilities you investigate.

Chapter Five

THE VALUE AND EFFICACY
OF 12-STEP PROGRAMS IN
TREATMENT
(Some frank words about AA, NA, and Al-Anon)

12-step programs do tremendous good. They help millions of people and provide support, structure, and stability to the lives of people seeking recovery from many different substances and behaviors. For numerous years, drug and alcohol treatment, specifically, used the 12-steps and 12-step programs as their sole curriculum. In the late 80s, recovering people used to joke that they'd just paid $8,000. for a copy of the Big book *(the affectionate term given to the book Alcoholics Anonymous)* and a ride to AA meetings for a month.

I am sure that these treatment centers did what they thought would work—what they thought would help addicts and alcoholics get well. I'm sure they had the best of intentions;

however, addicts and alcoholics always needed more than a Big Book and a ride to meetings. This approach, today, is as unethical as it is lazy. It comes from the uneducated opinions of people who have likely been in similar treatment programs themselves. I do not recommend considering a treatment center that has focused its program entirely on the 12-steps. If the daily program of activities consists of Big Book studies, 12-step studies, and sponsorship groups, it's not treatment! They are trying to sell you something that was given to the addiction community for free. There are no dues or fees for attending AA, NA, CA, CMA, Al-Anon, and the host of other anonymous programs.

Having said this, 12-step programs are essential, in my opinion, for long-term recovery. Clients, in treatment, need to be exposed to meetings on a daily basis, but they also need treatment! They need sponsors, but they also need professional staff that is well-educated in the field of addiction. *(Sponsors are members of 12-step organizations who have some significant time in sobriety and who make themselves available to help those, generally, newer in sobriety. They offer their experience, strength, and hope, along with taking these newer members through the 12 steps.)*

If you are seriously shopping for recovery programs suitable for yourself or someone you care about, research the staff, their levels of education, and their experience in the field.

Allusion to the 12-steps in treatment is not only important but unavoidable. In treatment, the goal is to demonstrate a model for living that clients can learn and then later adapt to their daily lives. Beginning the day with meditation—especially teaching different forms of meditation, is referencing the 11th step *(and it's a good living practice)*. In a similar fashion, ending the day with a period of reflection is pointing toward the 10th step *(and this is also an excellent way to go through life)*. Mentioning the hopelessness and despair that addiction inevitably brings is definitely 1st step material.

Furthermore, newly recovering addicts need to learn effective communication skills, how to become productive members of *(first their recovering community and later)* the larger community. They need useful coping techniques as well as guidance in how to begin a new life, centered in living meaningfully.

Another practice that has become prevalent in treatment facilities is sending heroin and methamphetamine addicts only to Alcoholics Anonymous meetings. What many of these facilities say is, "That's where the recovery is. There's no recovery in NA or CMA." This is simply not true. A good treatment center exposes its clients to several 12-step programs because: it is identification that is the key ingredient in the 12-step movement. Clients need to identify with the people in the various 12-step rooms. It is unlikely that a crack cocaine addict will fully relate or feel comfortable in a meeting designed for alcoholics and vice versa. The more accurate reason that those facilities send everyone to AA is convenience. At the very least, addiction treatment facilities should blend AA, NA, and Al-Anon, giving their clients an idea of what is actually available for them. It is the treatment center's responsibility to attend the meetings that they send their clients to. They should make sure that the meetings attended are healthy and have a balanced mix of clean time or sobriety. 12-step sponsorship should be sought from within the 12-step community and not from employees of the treatment center.

"What about the treatment centers that advertise not being 12-step. Do they offer valuable treatment?"

Many treatment centers choose not to involve their clients in any way with 12-step recovery. I surmise that much of this is simply a marketing ploy. Even so, I do realize that atheists are put off by the 12 steps, and they likely always will be *(due to references to God or Higher Power)*.

So it would appear that if these non-12-step rehabs are doing good therapeutic work, including psychiatry, nutrition, neurofeedback, trauma integration and life coaching in preparation for transitioning after treatment, they are needed.

However, there should always be some kind of peer support encouraged for those addicts, repelled by spiritual concepts. This should be a part of treatment, so the clients can be amongst their "people" and not tackle their addictions alone. There are three groups that do a good job in creating community for those not interested in attending 12-step programs.

Secular Organization for Sobriety *(SOS)* is a non-profit that has been around a long time and offers the kind of peer support that addicts need over the long haul. secularsobriety.org

Rational Recovery is a for-profit organization that can be found across the nation, serving those looking to maintain a sober way of life. rational.org

SMART Recovery *(Smart Management and Recovery Training)* is a nationwide not-for-profit organization that provides free self-help support groups to people who want to abstain from addictive behaviors. The site has online recovery meetings, a message board, Internet discussion groups, a meeting list and recommended reading. smartrecovery.org

Many agnostics and atheists have used the group itself as a "higher power" within the 12-step context. Not only that, those principles set down by secular humanists are indeed spiritual at their core. So, don't let rigidity and/or dogma stop you from finding a group of people, with whom you feel comfortable, and sticking around for a long time— perhaps even growing in a way that supports and uplifts others as well as yourself.

It is so easy to forget, after a period of years, that one has a problem with drugs or alcohol. Life gets busy, pressures and stress add up, and addicts, who are abstinent, relapse *(It would appear to be our default switch)*. One of the greatest rewards of long-term membership in a 12-step program is having a place to share wisdom with others and to simply be a survivor of this disease in a room with others, who "understand." There is abundant support in the 12-step rooms. And addicts should look for groups that give them a feeling of having just been served "soul food." To be explicit:

Experience, Wisdom, Compassion, Under-standing, Open-mindedness, and Love—

"I didn't have the problem. Why should I have to go to meetings?"

Al-Anon is a 12-step support group for the friends and family members of alcoholics *(Sons, daughters, mothers, husbands, wives, fathers, and coworkers).* Even so, Al-Anon welcomes those who have relationships with drug ad-dicts as well. They have years of tested experi-ence in living with the disease of addiction. Al-Anon helps to educate their members about the disease. They have excellent guidelines about what's helpful and not helpful, and rooms filled with people who have "been through it all." I cannot emphasize enough, how important I believe attending Al-Anon is for the loved ones of alcoholics and addicts. You may regain your sanity, and you will certainly gain a new per-spective about this disease *(and perhaps some inner peace, which has likely eluded you since you and the addiction first crossed paths).* Go to-night!

Chapter Six

MEDICATIONS—ABSOLUTELY!
Let the Medical Experts Treat this Disease

The importance of excellent addictionolo-gists and addiction-savvy psychiatrists cannot be overstated.

To be candid, I am not a doctor, nor do I purport to have an expertise in addiction medicine or psychopharmacology. There is a PDF available in the back of the book, with some excellent professional choices should you be in need of one.

I've been in the 12-step rooms and involved in drug treatment since the dark ages, and this is not simply a statement of time passing. This was a time, in the 1980s, when the field of addiction had not elevated its level of knowledge or understanding to where it is today. And it was not even in the ball park. You could call my beginnings, both personal and professional, "old school." We often participated in "cold turkey" detoxifications, falsely believing that the degree of discomfort someone experienced would add to his or her desire to stay clean over the long haul. Benzodiazepines were administered to alcoholics for brief periods of time because there was knowledge that detoxing from heavy drinking could lead to seizures and/or fatalities. Centers used Antabuse and alcohol together, in order to dissuade alcoholics from drinking. Additionally, there was enormous controversy about taking any psychotropic medications and claiming to be clean and sober; although treatment centers were beginning to prescribe antidepressants to some clients.

Sorrowfully, I was a part of this "uneducated," misinformed era, based on no medical training or informed research whatsoever. I admit this here to make the bold statement: "I was wrong, as were many of my colleagues."

Alcohol and drug treatment centers were the first to change, and then the various 12-step rooms came around over time. *(It has always been the official position of 12-step programs, at their organizational levels, that people take their medications as prescribed. Anonymous societies consider the medical profession to be the experts—and the debate was always an outside issue of which they had no organized opinion.*

However, there have been many opinionated members who've made it harder for people to get well and stay well.)

Today, we know a great deal more about addiction and co-occurring issues such as depression, anxiety, ADD/ADHD, and others. Previously these issues played a great role in addicts being unable to accomplish and maintain their sobriety. There was an extensive push in the 1990s to treat that minority of patients who suffered from dual diagnosis *(the name given to the co-occurring issues listed above).* It's been my observation, along with many addictionologists that I've spoken with, that all addicts are dually diagnosed. In fact, I believe these states are primary precursors to the addiction itself.

Addictionologists are adept at recognizing the depressive states that accompany opiate addiction, the anxiety that's always present in alcoholism, and the high numbers of amphetamine addicts who have relatively severe ADD/ADHD. They are able to competently medicate these primary issues that addicts have been trying to medicate through illicit drug use. And helping addicts to achieve more balanced brain chemistry is an essential beginning in long-term recovery.

Treating these conditions, including bipolar disorder, is imperative for addicts to have the optimum chance of achieving lasting sobriety.

Today, we advocate giving addicts safe, comfortable and medically-supervised detoxifications. Allowing addicts to suffer the pains of withdrawal is not only unnecessary, it is ill-advised. So please make sure that if you or your loved one is addicted to opiates, alcohol, or benzodiazepines—a medically safe detox is part of your initial treatment experience. Most treatment centers today offer this, but make sure the one you're considering does.

For years, about the only two anti-addiction medications were Disulfiram *(Antabuse)* and Methadone. Antabuse, which creates an unpleasant reaction when drinking alcohol and therefore reduces the compulsion to drink, has been a drug of some controversy *(over its effectiveness for treating alcoholism)* because alcoholics will not volitionally continue to take it. Methadone is a synthetic opioid. It is typically used by patients with opiate addiction to taper off narcotics through withdrawal-avoidance and maintenance. This drug, too, has been controversial due to its basis in harm-reduction rather than complete abstinence. Even so, when looked at as a chronic disease, helping IV drug addicts to avoid HIV infections, overdoses, illicit drug activities—including criminal behaviors and suicides, it is a valid form of treatment. Not only that, there are many addicts who are able to make the leap from Methadone maintenance to full recovery over time.

Some of the best news today is: we have excellent medications to aide in addiction recovery. The research for Suboxone has been both substantial and impressive. It is a combination of buprenorphine and naloxone. Buprenorphine *(Subutex)* combined with Naloxone create Suboxone. Suboxone is used to treat opioid dependence *(addiction to opioid drugs, including heroin and narcotic painkillers)*. Buprenorphine is in a class of medications called opioid partial agonist-antagonists, and naloxone is in a class of medications called opioid antagonists. The combination of buprenorphine and naloxone prevent withdrawal symptoms when someone stops taking opioid drugs while still producing similar effects to these drugs. Suboxone is used over months to help opiate addicts slowly taper down to nothing. However, many sober living and transitional living facilities will not take addicts who are on Suboxone, which is still a matter of prejudice and ignorance. The current research shows the best results for opiate recovery is Suboxone over a 6 to 12 month period. Stopping the treatment prematurely is not advisable. So in making decisions about treatment, look ahead to a year in the future. Ideally, the opiate addict would be able to taper off Suboxone with medical supervision and have several months off of it with the support of a recovery community.

Naltrexone is an opioid receptor antagonist used primarily in the management of alcohol dependence and opioid dependence. It blocks the receptors in the pleasure centers of the brain that respond to alcohol and opiates. Even so, in pill form, it must be taken every day or its effects diminish. The use of Vivitrol is becoming more and more pervasive in treatment, which is a good thing. Vivitrol is primarily Naltrexone in an injectable form, given every four weeks. Many addictionologists prefer Vivitrol to Disulfiram for the treatment of alcoholism and suggest that in cases of opioid addiction, it's an ideal follow-up to appropriate Suboxone treatment. Please explore the treatment centers that you're considering and be assured that they have medical addiction specialists to assess either your needs or your loved one's needs. These medications have been available for many years; however, the addiction treatment field has taken a long time to catch up.

Campral *(acamprosate calcium)* is the most recent medication approved for the treatment of alcohol dependence or alcoholism in the United States, and it was approved by the Food and Drug Administration in 2004; however, Campral has been used widely in Europe for many years. It is estimated that more than 1.5 million people have been treated across the world. Scientists don't know exactly how Campral works in the brain to help alcoholics maintain abstinence or sobriety, yet it is believed to restore the chemical balance in the brain that has been disrupted by long-term or chronic alcoholism. In a nutshell, it would appear that Campral assists the brain to begin functioning normally again.

Intravenous nutrition therapy is often an excellent medical treatment choice because losses of vital nutrients are part and parcel in alcoholism and drug addiction. Vitamins, minerals and other nutrients can be helpful, in high concentrations, for healing the effects of addiction. By infusing the bloodstream with a concentrated dose of nutrients, the cells have rapid access to the very nutrients they require for getting better sooner. These vitamins and minerals may otherwise not be available because of poor diet, poor nutrient absorption and other reasons. Nutrients used in IV therapy include high doses of Vitamin C, Vitamin B12, B complex, thiamin, magnesium, calcium, zinc, selenium, alpha lipoic acid, and glutathione. The research shows that alcoholics given IV therapy tend to regain cognitive functioning much more rapidly than without the treatment. And let's face it, addicts and alcoholics alike are suffering from poor nutritional backgrounds, which does affect overall cognitive and physical functioning. If you are investigating facilities that offer IV vitamin/mineral therapies, please be certain that the treatments are overseen by a physician. I believe that we will see more addiction facilities adding this to their treatment modalities soon, as it is growing in popularity and efficacy.

Ibogaine, an ancient natural tribal remedy, originated from the Tabernanthe Iboga shrub native to Gabon and other nations in West Central Africa. Ibogaine has been used in shamanic ceremonies for possibly hundreds of years. More recently *(since the early 1960s)*, it has been thought that Ibogaine interrupts the addiction process. Those countries that utilize it *(many countries do not because of its psychoactive properties)* report impressive results with the use of this natural extract. Treatment centers in Mexico and Costa Rica report that addicts can experience symptom-free withdrawals and a physiological release from their addictions. This said, addicts struggle with how to live once they've gotten off drugs. This is why there are so many reports of relapse after Ibogaine treatment. If this is an addiction remedy you choose, I would highly recommend at least a 90 day treatment stay, in the United States, in order to address important life skills and valuable tools for living meaningfully in recovery.

Chapter Seven

SPIRITUALITY
The Essence of Living a Meaningful Life—
Recovery 101

Finding a place to begin, when discussing spirituality, is a daunting task. I've spent the majority of my life on a path of discovery, looking for truths, untruths, inner knowledge, and connection with God. I'm using the word God, throughout this chapter, because it's a word that everyone can represent within his or her own psyche. For some, he is male *(in fact, he is an old, white male with long white hair, and a long white beard).* For others, God is woman—Goddess. There are those who believe God is the creative intelligence throughout the universe *(or multiverse, depending on your point of view).* And still others who depend on the fundamental nature of God to be love. Some humanize God to represent themselves, and many—too many in my opinion, fear God.

The Dalai Lama has said, "I always tell my western friends that it is best to keep your own tradition. Changing Religion is not easy and sometimes causes confusion. You must value your tradition and honor your own religion."

He has a great point. There is wisdom in beginning where you are *(of blooming where you're planted so to speak)*. Even so, many have resentment toward the religious teachings of their backgrounds. There are those who have no spiritual history to speak of and multitudes of seekers, looking for truths beyond what they have been offered. This chapter is not about religion—it's about the truths behind the great religions—the mystical sects in all of them. And the messages of true love, tolerance, and forgiveness found throughout religion if one looks for them. If you are angry with your religion of origin, this might be the perfect place to begin. Your practice could be a letting go of hostility and resentment—allowing what is to simply be.

A spiritual tenet that deserves special attention, especially for those in recovery, is to let go of grievances or resentments. This is pivotal because one cannot live peacefully or lovingly if he or she is riddled with long-held hostility toward others. This aspect of personal growth really matters in choosing to live "a spiritual life."

There are many paths to letting go of resentments. One of them is found within the 12 Steps.

It helps to take a good look at our own lives, and see that no matter what we have done, it was the best we could do at the time. Now here is the hard part: This adage is equally true for everyone—absolutely everyone. Can you now practice making space for that within yourself and then for others?

Quieting the mind is a fundamental part of every spiritual tradition. Through meditation, centering prayer, running, singing, chanting, or coloring mandalas—find a practice that quiets the mind, and practice it each day. There are teachers and coaches for every form of meditation and practice that exists. When you discover one that interests you, deepen it with a solid teacher.

Not listening to the random thoughts that come and go throughout the day, every day is an art, but it is an art worth cultivating. We "make up" more reasons to be hurt, sad, and angry than actual events create.

Beyond not carrying resentment, is the practice of not gossiping. Gossiping is carrying negative tales *(true, untrue, or unknown)* to others for the titillating experience of having information that someone else wants. It's noxious, and gossip destroys people. In the Jewish tradition, it's equivalent to murder *(The murder of character)*. Even if a story is true *(which we rarely know)*, when we spread it to others, the "offenders" don't have a chance to change and grow. Their negative image becomes indelibly retained by those we've shared the information with. When we cease the practice of poisoning the river before others, we are well on our way to living a spiritual life.

Telling the truth with a kind and compassionate heart—being authentic with all people in all circumstances is another way to grow spiritually. This is not as easy as it sounds, especially for those of the addictive persuasion. Addicts and alcoholics are often chameleon types. They change their personalities *(to some degree)*, depending upon who they are with. Becoming who you really are and beginning to let go of the need for others' love or approval is a spiritual feat. Keep practicing. You are worth it!

Leading a life of service is a practice that many have found to be fulfilling and pivotal to their own spiritual growth. This is also a process that takes time to unravel and understand. It's important here to be of service from the heart and not out of guilt and obligation. It can be tedious to discern the difference. Try it on for size anyway. Look for service that matches your heart. If you don't know what's in your heart, think about the things, people, and issues that make you cry. That's a good beginning.

Don't avoid what's happening in your life. Don't run away. It could be an initiation or a lesson from God. What's happening in your life is what's in front of you. Take it head on. Leap forward. Make big mistakes. But don't run away from the issues that are presented to you. This one thing could transform your life. Be with what is—explore it. See what you can learn about yourself and others. Nobody gets closer to God, the truth, or themselves by running away from or avoiding the unpleasantries within his or her life.

Practice non-hatred if you can't practice love. Start here. The Buddhists have a beautiful practice in this direction. It's the compassion meditation: I site this specifically because the results from the practice are palpable.

Begin by envisioning yourself in your mind's eye—stay there until you can clearly see yourself, now say: "I wish you happiness and the root of happiness. I wish you the end of suffering and the root of suffering."

This practice presumes the idea that happiness is a byproduct of living a meaningful life—and that all suffering comes from ignorance and false beliefs.

Now find someone you love—picture them, and wish them "happiness and the root of happiness, as well as the end of suffering and the root of suffering."

At this point, find a person you like and repeat the exercise. Next, seek out a person you have neither positive feelings for nor negative feelings for—wish them "happiness and the root of happiness—and the end of suffering and the root of suffering"

You're doing great! I want you to find a person you don't like much, see them in your mind's eye, and repeat the exercise.

This time, seek out a person or group that you hate; see this person or group clearly, and wish this person or group "happiness and the root of happiness, along with the end of suffering and the root of suffering."

Close the exercise with you again, repeat, "I wish you happiness and the root of happiness. I wish you the end of suffering and the root of suffering."

It becomes clear that if people lived meaningful lives they would be happy and thereby transformed. It also becomes self-evident that if people were not befuddled by false beliefs, they would not suffer—this includes all of us.

An old phrase applies here: Hurt people hurt people. This is where compassion and open-heartedness begin, making space for those that you've hurt and those who have hurt you.

Read something uplifting and heart-opening every day. Spend 10 minutes each day, enlarging your thinking. It truly matters what we put into our heads. You can easily give a few minutes each day toward this end, and prayer is a beautiful practice.

Find prayers that speak to your heart. Or when you pray, be honest. Come to God with the totality of you. Work toward connection and peace.

I've included my favorite books on prayer, meditation, and spiritual practice in the back of the book. Search them out and find your teachers. Not everyone is your teacher, so find those who touch you deeply.

Spirituality is a life-long proposition; and in my opinion, one cannot have a peaceful, lasting sobriety without it. Practice every day, and you'll be surprised at how your levels of happiness and serenity grow.

Meister Eckhart suggested that, "If the only prayer you said was thank you, that would be enough." And that's another place to begin.

Chapter Eight

HOW TO GET WELL AND STAY WELL—IN SPITE OF OURSELVES

Alright, we're down to it. Here's the secret. Trust that your addiction has turned on you because it has. There is no going back. It will never get better or go back to the way it once was. If you're in the legal system—if you are in treatment—if you are filled with shame and remorse, this is as good as it gets from now on. From this point forward, it will always get worse when you use. I understand what an incredible betrayal this is—like losing the friend you could always count on; and yet, that friend is lost. It left you to die, humiliated, broken, bleeding, and alone.

You're going to need help. And the good news is: help is available. At the very least, go to a 12-step meeting right now. Ask your family for help getting you into treatment. Get on the N.I.D.A. website and find a treatment center near you. Call the locally listed numbers for AA or NA. Talk to someone. Everyone who answers the phone is in recovery themselves. They answer the phone in order to talk with you. If you're one of us, you are never alone. That can be a daunting proposition, but you are about to become a member of one of the largest secret societies in existence. We're all over the world.

When you get help, do what they tell you to do. That's right. It sounds crazy I know... But surrender to the idea that you have lost your mind in the pursuit of alcohol and drugs. Everything healthy will sound foreign and outrageous to you. That's OK. Do the healthy thing anyway. You're going to have to trust something besides yourself for a while. So I want you to trust the people who have come before you. They know the road and will not take you too far off the path, even with their human imperfections.

If the doctor recommends medication, take it. If you have to get up at 6:30 in the morning, set your alarm. When they force you to go to groups, participate. Practice the habits of being honest and authentic. Remember, this will take a lot of practice but don't stop trying. Find a sponsor who has taken the steps and who has a good life. Listen to that sponsor and do what he or she suggests, especially when you don't want to. Begin meditating. Start where you are at and investigate new forms that appeal to you. Try everything. Discover things to be grateful for *(for instance—you get a second chance at life)*. Look for the good in people; you will find what you look for. This will always be true.

See what you can add to the river of life. Practice humility *(Humility is not thinking less of yourself, it's thinking of yourself less)*. Try on spiritual paths. If you are fortunate enough to get therapy and neurofeedback, attend your sessions. Be willing—be willing— be willing. If you are in treatment, create a sober contract with your therapist and family *(see appendix A in the back of the book)*. One day it might save your life.

Over time, get yourself in the center of the heard *(surrounded by those recovering people who have done it longer than you have)*. It's harder to get picked off that way. Practice loving the people in recovery and then practice loving yourself. Love is a verb *(a series of actions taken or not taken in the direction of growth, support, and wellbeing for who you are, and everyone else truly is)*.

Give some time and energy away. Be of ser- vice. Get a job. Find a better job. If you are looking to do something else, go to school. In fact, the Federal Department of Rehabilitation will pay for your retraining, as an addict in recovery *(at least for a while longer—budget-cuts notwithstanding)*. When they ask you if you have other issues, the answer is "yes." Get a letter from your doctor, psychiatrist, or therapist. You are the reason why we have this agency, and you deserve a new beginning.

Continue practicing honesty, willingness, and open-mindedness. Learn about loving kindness and compassion. Compassion comes from pain, so you are already a natural. Look for heroes. If you're in a 12-step program, for God's sake, take the steps. They are principles that have been time-tested in all of the mystical traditions, besides being really good ideas. Exercise. Eat well and invest in your physical condition. When you feel better, life is a little easier. Remember that no matter what occurs, there are others who have been through it before you and who will share their experiences with you.

Don't avoid people or uncomfortable situations. Avoidance is running away from important learning opportunities. What you avoid will come back to you again and again. So tackle those things head on. Do your damnedest. Make mistakes but don't run. Life has never been easy, not since the beginning of time. Acceptance of this can play a large role in successful recovery. It rains on the using and the clean and sober, but sober, you've got tools with which to find the umbrella.

Develop a sense of humor. Laugh. See comedies and express joy. Try not to take things so seriously. Learn to tell jokes. Find interesting people from whom you can learn something new. Let that be a new practice for you. Get to know folks. Take time in solitude while also engaging with others. Try to let go of those things or people you've deluded yourself into thinking "you have to have in order to be happy or stay sober." You don't.

Explore not holding grievances—they are not helpful to you or the rest of us.

Put your spiritual life on an equal footing with your sobriety—they are connected, and you can't have one without the other. Do these things to the best of your ability, and you will do well. If you should relapse, get help again. Don't fall into the pit of shame for having a disease that you didn't ask for, but make sure to get help. And after you get help, do what they tell you to do, as unnatural as it seems.

We are all here to help you. Don't ever forget it. When you are ready, you'll join us in being here to help the next one down the pike. It's a peculiar special purpose, but our people need us.

Finally, as much as you can, stay in today. Just for today, you have everything you need, and that will never change.

Appendix A
Sober Contract

Your life is important! I/We will support you 100% in the direction of your sobriety, health, wellness, and life. However, I/We will not give $5.00 or 5 minutes toward your addiction, your self-destruction, or your ultimate death. To be clear, count on me/us to be behind you every step of the way, as you rebuild your life. But should you relapse, my/our support will be limited to getting you immediately back into treatment—Period. You are that important to me/us.

_____ *(Family initials here)*

_____

Should you have a relapse (if the cancer returns), this is what all of us have agreed to:

on, _____, ___. *(Date)*

_____You go immediately back into treatment *(if the treatment was 30 days previously, this time it's 90 days—If it was 90 days previously, this time it is 6 months) (Client initials here)*

_____There will be no enabling you, should you make the poor choice to leave treatment early. I/We will not come and get you or send you money. There will be no coming home until you've completed your treatment. *(All initial here)*

_____When your treatment is complete, you will move into a transitional living facility (for a minimum of 90 days) where you can gain support in building a new life in recovery. *(Client initials here)*

_____You agree to see both an addictionologist and a licensed therapist, after leaving treatment and upon returning home. *(Client initials here)*

_____You agree to continue going to 12-step meetings each week, getting a sponsor, and attending a home group. *(Client initials here)*

_____I/We agree to attend Al-Anon each week and to learn about living successfully with the disease of addiction. *(Family Initials here)*

_____We agree (as a couple or a family) to attend couples or family therapy, to repair any damage that we have done to each other. *(All initial here)*

You are not alone in this illness. I/We love you, and will not leave you to face this on your own. With all of my/our heart/s, I/we want you to thrive and to live a meaningful, happy life. It is to this end, that together, we develop a plan for your healing.

_____ _____
Signature of Client   *Date*

_____ _____
Signature of Wife/Husband *Date*

_____ _____
Signature of Family Member *Date*

_____ _____
Signature of Witness   *Date*

I recommend that everyone in treatment work with his/her therapist and family to develop such a plan. Remember that the dosage of treatment should go up, not down, in instances of relapse. Of course this contract can be changed to meet the individual therapeutic needs of each client. But it is better to do this while someone is in treatment, before being crippled by the mental effects of a relapse.

Appendix B
Books to Support a
New Life

These are some of my favorites: I hope you will find great joy in them…

Books from the 12-Step Tradition:

Alcoholics Anonymous

The Twelve Steps and Twelve Traditions

The Language of the Heart

As Bill Sees It

The Search For Serenity by Lewis F. Presnall

A New Pair of Glasses by Chuck C.

The Narcotics Anonymous Basic Text

NA: It Works—How and Why

52 Weeks of Esteemable Acts: A Guide to Right Living by Francine Ward

Not God by Ernest Kurtz

The Spirituality of Imperfection by Ernest Kurtz

One Breath at a Time: Buddhism and the 12 Steps by Kevin Griffin

12 Steps on Buddha's Path: Bill, Buddha, and We by Laura S.

Realm of the Hungry Ghosts by Gabor Mate

Denial is not a River in Egypt by Sandi Bachom

The Wide Open Door by Tav Sparks

Al-Anon Paths to Recovery

Al-Anon Twelve Steps and Twelve Traditions

The Language of Letting Go by Melodie Beattie

Books from the Christian Tradition:

Hinds Feet On High Places by Hannah Hurnard

Mountains and Spices by Hannah Hurnard

The Sermon on the Mount by Emmet Fox

My Utmost for His Highness by Oswald Chambers

Surprised By Joy by C.S. Lewis

The Seven Storey Mountain by Thomas Merton

No Man is an Island by Thomas Merton

New Seeds of Contemplation by Thomas Merton

Thoughts in Solitude by Thomas Merton

Wisdom in the Desert by Thomas Merton

Awareness: the perils and opportunities of reality by Anthony de Mello

Awakening: conversations with the masters by Anthony de Mello

Writings by Anthony de Mello

The Way to Love by Anthony de Mello

Grace Eventually by Anne Lamott

Plan B. Further Thoughts on Faith by Anne Lamott

Traveling Mercies by Anne Lamott

Help, Thanks, Wow by Anne Lamott

Stitches: a handbook on meaning, hope, and repair by Anne Lamott

Peace of Heart by St. Francis of Assisi

Padre Pio: the true story by C. Bernard Ruffin

Return to Love by Marianne Williamson

Everyday Grace by Marianne Williamson

Illuminata by Marianne Williamson

Practicing the Presence by Joel Goldsmith

Consciousness Transformed by Joel Goldsmith

Good Spiritual Thought:

The Four Agreements by don Miguel Ruiz

The Fifth Agreement by don Miguel Ruiz and don Jose Ruiz

The Mastery of Love by don Miguel Ruiz

The Mastery of Fear by don Miguel Ruiz

Loving What is by Byron Katie

A Thousand Names for Joy by Byron Katie

Who Would You Be Without Your Story by Byron Katie

I Need Your Love is That True by Byron Katie

The Power of Now by Eckhart Tolle

A New Earth by Eckhart Tolle

Be Here Now by Ram Das

The Journey of Awakening by Ram Das

I'm Still Here by Ram Das

How Can I Help? by Ram Das

A Course In Miracles by the Foundation of Inner Peace

Love is Letting Go of Fear by Gerald Jampolsky

Life's Operating Manual by Tom Shadyac

The Disappearance of the Universe by Gary Renard

The Dude and the Zen Master by Jeff Bridges and Bernie Glassman

Dharma Punx by Noah Levine

Against the Stream by Noah Levine

The Heart of the Revolution by Noah Levine

Jonathon Livingston Seagull by Richard Bach

Illusions by Richard Bach

When Things Fall Apart by Pema Chödrön

The Places That Scare You by Pema Chödrön

Download a Free Resource Guide
from the Author

visit:

www.illustrationbrain.com/rehab

This guide includes a list of the Author's recommended addiction treatment centers and addiction treatment professionals.

About the Author

In recovery for over 25 years, Janice Witt has been helping other addicts and alcoholics get well for nearly 24 of them. Janice's most recent children's books are *Harold: a very long dog with a very big heart* and *Harold- Discovers Santa's Secret*. Her collaboration with writer Pete Stewart should be out in 2014—*Terminally Unique: the stories of two addicts, their ravaged lives, and their paths back to grace*

Janice Witt was first published in the Pearl Literary Journal in 1989. She has spent years writing and reading as a featured artist at various coffee houses and galleries, including Johnny Otis' "Art of the Spoken word" in Sebastopol, California. She has written for both the Topanga Messenger and Women's Voices.

Janice published her book of poetry: *Romance and Other Humiliations from a Texas Waitress with Heartworm*: Iguana Press/1990 and has been seen in Louder Than Bombs and Feh: the journal of odious poetry, among others.

Made in the USA
San Bernardino, CA
20 December 2013